Mary H. Page

**Graded Schools in the United States of America**

Mary H. Page

**Graded Schools in the United States of America**

ISBN/EAN: 9783337834975

Printed in Europe, USA, Canada, Australia, Japan

Cover: Foto ©Paul-Georg Meister /pixelio.de

More available books at **www.hansebooks.com**

# GRADED SCHOOLS

## IN THE

# UNITED STATES OF AMERICA

BY

## MARY H. PAGE

*Head Mistress of the Skinners' School, Stamford Hill*

𝕷𝖔𝖓𝖉𝖔𝖓

## SWAN SONNENSCHEIN & CO

NEW YORK: MACMILLAN & CO.

1894

# PREFACE

In view of the growing interest in Secondary Education in the United Kingdom and the important problems awaiting solution, the Gilchrist Trustees decided in the early part of 1893 to send five women teachers to America, for the purpose of studying and reporting upon Secondary Schools for Girls and Institutions for the Training of Women in different parts of the States. The Trustees made their intention widely known, and invited the governing bodies of the various women's colleges and associations of teachers to submit to them names of persons specially qualified. The Trustees received in this way a list of some of the ablest and most experienced women teachers in the country. After careful consideration of the qualifications of the numerous candidates, the Trustees selected the following five, and awarded to each of them a travelling scholarship of £100 to enable them to spend two months in the 'United States in prosecuting their investigations:—Miss A. Bramwell, B.Sc. (Lecturer at the Cambridge Training College), Miss

iii

S. A. Burstall, B.A. (Mistress at the North London Collegiate School for Girls), Miss H. M. Hughes (Principal of the Women's Training Department, University College, Cardiff), Miss M. H. Page (Head Mistress of the Skinners' Company's School for Girls, Stamford Hill), and Miss A. Zimmern (Mistress at the High School for Girls, Tunbridge Wells). The five scholars visited America during last summer, and presented to the Trustees carefully prepared Reports, of which one—viz., that by Miss Page—is presented to the public in this volume. The Trustees have aided in the publication of these Reports, because they believe that a knowledge of the educational systems and experiments which have been tried by the English-speaking people over the Atlantic cannot fail to be of interest and value to those engaged in attempting to solve the educational problems of the United Kingdom.

R. D. ROBERTS,
*Secretary to the Gilchrist*
*Trustees.*

17, VICTORIA STREET,
WESTMINSTER.

# INTRODUCTION

THE following brief Report of the work undertaken by me through the help of the Trustees of the Gilchrist Educational Trust has of necessity been written hurriedly, in the midst of the daily pressure of heavy work; and is, I feel, totally inadequate either to show the benefit I have personally received or to give anything like a systematic account of Education in America.

Travelling from the Atlantic to the Pacific, as far north as Montreal and as far south as St. Louis, I felt again and again that to know American Education would need more years of study than I had months in which to see and to hear. A Western State I found to be a different country from an Eastern State; the former seemed bound by no traditions, governed by no conventionalities, narrowed or hampered by no class feeling, whether as regards people or work; and as " necessity is the mother of invention," so a new State evidently must be the parent of fresh experiment in every profession, business, or trade.

The whole country is so huge, the possibilities so enormous, and the resulting conditions so diverse, that beyond the broad principles of government which underlie the organizations of education, I have found it impossible to give generalizations.

I felt, both before starting and increasingly during my tour, that statistics were cold and hard, and although very necessary in their place, were not the main points for me to seek out in a visit.  I therefore endeavoured to enter into the life which is being lived in the Schools, to realize where possible the actual difficulties to be contended with, and the aims kept in view by superintendents and teachers; and while I visited schools so far as time and strength would allow, I attached more importance to interviews with superintendents, teachers, and secretaries, than to cursory inspection of schools.

At the close of my Report, I append a list, but by no means an exhaustive list, of the schools and institutions I visited, and of those friends who so kindly gave me their time and much valuable information; and if ever this Report should reach their eyes, I should be glad for them to know how much I appreciated the generous way in which they so liberally placed their time at my disposal. Especially have I cause to thank Dr. Harris, the United States Commissioner of Education, Professor Spice, of

Brooklyn, and Miss Cropsey, of Indianapolis, for the courteous and untiring aid they rendered me, and Professor Fitzpatrick, Superintendent of Omaha City Schools (Nebraska), for the exceedingly kind way in which he helped me, not only in educational matters with advice and introductions both in the Eastern and Western States of America, but also as regards routes of travelling, and many other details which are so frequently causes of hindrance to a traveller in a strange land.

As regards the introductions kindly given by Dr. Fitch, I much regret that I was personally unfortunate. With but a few exceptions, the friends were away from their homes at the times of my visits.

I propose in the following Report merely to state, in as concise and connected a form as I can, those facts which came directly under my own cognizance, particularly as Dr. Fitch has so admirably stated the general laws of government in his "Notes on American Schools and Colleges," of which book one School Superintendent remarked to me, "It is the best and most correct account of our American education given by an outsider." But, although I feel I cannot attempt any general account of the system of education in America, I also feel that a few words in reference to it are necessary, in order to make intelligible the School expressions which I shall be obliged to use.

Education in the United States is national in the sense of being provided for by the laws and of drawing support from the taxes, but there is no federal system of education, only "a number of separate systems. Each State has its own educational laws, and raises, appropriates, and distributes school funds in its own way."

"In one respect only has the Central Government concerned itself with education. In 1785 it was ordained that in all new States hereafter to be added to the seventeen then existing, a special appropriation of one-sixteenth of the public land should be reserved for the purpose of supplying a school fund. There are now forty-two States in the American Union, but many of them sold the lands in order to defray the initial charge of erecting schools, and comparatively few now enjoy the rent or use it as a permanent revenue for maintenance of the schools.

"They all require further aid from State or local taxation. The State of Indiana has the distinction of having husbanded its resources with exceptional discretion and ability." — "Notes on American Schools and Colleges," pp. 15, 16.

Each State has its own State Superintendent of Education, and he usually appoints the County Superintendents. The business of the County Superintendent is to divide the county into school districts according to the population of that part, and to arrange generally for the education of the county. But the State delegates to cities the control of their own schools; hence the schools in two cities in the same State may be as different in detail as are the schools of two different States. Nevertheless, I found a certain amount of uniformity in all the schools that I visited. All have the Primary Grades passing on to the Grammar Grades, and above the Grammar Grades the High Schools, which last may lead to college life, but may also lead to business life.

The term "school" is used in America in two senses, first as the building, second as we use the word form or class.

"Grammar School" is an historical term; and, though it has lost its old meaning, which came from the old English Grammar Schools, it is retained in use.

The following was my route :—

New York, Brooklyn, Vassar, Springfield, Northampton (Smith College), Boston (Wellesley College), Philadelphia, Baltimore, Washington, Indianapolis, St. Louis, Kansas City, Leavenworth, Omaha, Denver, Bonanza, Manitou, Tacoma, Seattle, New Westminster, Winnipeg, Chicago, Niagara, Toronto, Montreal, New York.

In conclusion, I venture to add that only one who

has been able to enjoy the privilege of travelling over some previously unknown country, with the definite purpose of observing and studying the methods, manners, and effects of the education of that country, can at all realize the enormous amount of benefit given and received by such generous Travelling Scholarships as those offered last year by the Trustees of the Gilchrist Educational Trust.

MARY H. PAGE.

# CONTENTS

xi

# The Graded Schools in the United States.

*General Plan of Work.*

As the work I especially undertook in connection with the Gilchrist Scholarship was the study of the Graded Schools, at each place I visited I sought first the School superintendent, and learning from him which were the most typical schools, visited them; afterwards, in so far as time allowed, visiting hap-hazard any schools which I might pass, and then comparing them with the schools specially recommended. By this means I was enabled to see those schools in which the special aims of the superintendent were presumably carried out according to his wishes, and also schools in which the principals were less fortunate. Some general points struck me in these visits.

B

*Nationality.*

The evident desire to cultivate in the children the idea that they are but individuals of one nation—and that a very great nation. This seemed to me to be evident in the way in which the children are marshalled together to pass out of the building in regiments; the way in which lessons in civil government are given, by which the duties of a citizen are inculcated into the minds of the pupils; and the way in which the special national holidays are utilised, by being made show days for the school children, and oration days for their benefit.

On one occasion — " Commemoration Day " — I was present at the ceremony.

The children—boys and girls together—marched out to the drums beaten by some of their own number, then filed past the school building, where a large concourse of people were assembled, paused to sing National songs, listened to a stirring oration from an old soldier as to the bravery of the soldiers who fell on both sides in the war between the North and the South, and whose fall they were "commemorating," and, finally, after a National song sung in full chorus, the children departed to carry wreaths and baskets of flowers wherewith to decorate the graves of those soldiers who were buried in their immediate vicinity.

In many States they celebrate " Arbor Day," by way, of calling attention to the trees of their country, and encouraging care and love for them.

I give the following extracts from the "Arbor Day" circular issued by J. F. Crooker, Esq., School Superintendent at Albany.

"Chapter 196.

"*An Act to Encourage Arboriculture.*

"Approved, *April* 30, 1888.

" The people of the State of New York, represented in Senate and Assembly, do enact as follows :—

" *Section* 1.—-The Friday following the first day of May, in each year, shall hereafter be known throughout this State as Arbor Day.

" *Section* 2.—It shall be the duty of the authorities of every public school in this State to assemble the scholars in their charge on that day in the school building, or elsewhere, as they may deem proper, and to provide for and conduct—under the general supervision of the city superintendent or the school commissioner, or other chief officers having the general oversight of the public schools in each city or district—such exercise as shall tend to encourage the planting, protection, and preservation of trees and shrubs, and an acquaintance with the best methods to be adopted to accomplish such results.

"*Section* 3.—The State Superintendent of Public Instruction shall have power to prescribe from time to time, in writing, a course of exercises and instruction in the subjects hereinbefore mentioned, which shall be adopted and observed by the public school authorities on Arbor Day; and upon receipt of copies of such course, sufficient in number to supply all the schools under their supervision, the school commissioner or city superintendent aforesaid, shall promptly provide each of the schools under his or their charge with a copy, and cause it to be adopted and observed.

"*Section* 4.—This Act shall take effect immediately."

" *Arbor Day*, 1893.

" State of New York,

" Department of Public Instruction,

" Superintendent's Office,

" Albany, *March* 15, 1893.

" Dear Boys and Girls of our Public Schools,—

" Another spring is almost upon us, and we shall soon be called to celebrate the anniversary of that day which should bring to each one of us so much of happiness, for Nature will then be putting on her fresh green gown, as though preparing for a holiday, and we cannot help being glad and gay if we will but look for the joyousness and gaiety that are on every side of us. How beautifully it has been said of Nature—

' 'Tis her privilege,
Through all the years of this our life, to lead
From joy to joy.'

Listen for it in the freshening breezes that whisper stories of a happier time to come, and read it in the opening buds and blossoms that reveal a multitude of secrets.

" I would urge you, my dear young friends, to keep your eyes open this year for all those wonders of Nature which so many people pass by with

careless eye, never dreaming of the beauties that
might be disclosed if they would but attend.
Very true are the words of Ruskin: 'There is
not a moment of any day of our lives when
Nature is not producing scene after scene, picture
after picture, glory after glory, and working still
upon such exquisite and constant principles of the
most perfect beauty, that it is quite certain it is all
done for us, and intended for our perpetual plea-
sure.' How few persons recognise the charm of our
woods in early spring, when the first flush of wood-
land beauty appears to greet the smiling sun, when
our trees put on that variety and harmony of
apparel to celebrate the return of the spring. Do
you know what trees bud earliest? and did you ever
see the tiny early flowers of the maples and the
elms? Observe this year the first tree to bud and
blossom, and make a note of the tree and the date;
then follow this up with others in their turn. It
is surprising how little most persons really know
about the trees among which they have lived from
childhood. What in Nature ought to demand more
attention from us than trees, in being everywhere present—of large size, of picturesque appearance and of general usefulness?

" If you cannot all become accomplished scientists in this line, it is at least possible for every one to become interested in and acquainted with the trees in his neighbourhood.

" I would recommend to your attention this year a thorough and careful study of our maples. Let me urge you to study up the question of forestry ; be instrumental in helping along this great cause. Those who live in or near farms in the vicinity of woods or forests should have a watchful eye in regard to forest fires, which are most frequently started on farms, and every year burn tens of thousands of acres of forest land in the United States. Be practical in this work.

" Our prosperity is dependent, in a large degree, upon the preservation of our forests. A good forest is only an aggregated mass of trees. When we, as a people, come to know and appreciate and love trees, we shall learn to love forests too ; and once loving them, we shall appreciate their value ; and efforts to preserve and maintain them and to make them useful and productive for all time will then be a comparatively easy task ; but to do this you, my young friends, must grow up to love them and to appreciate their value.

"Perhaps you do not realize how much foreign governments are doing to preserve their forests, and how largely forests affect the rainfall, the climate and the river courses of a country. Some of our western States have awakened to these facts, and are putting forth great efforts in forest-tree planting ; Nebraska particularly, so that she who was once 'the treeless State' has become the pioneer State in this great work, and is now thickly studded with young forests, the result of setting out from eighteen to twenty millions of forest trees a year.

"It was a resident of Nebraska, Mr. J. Sterling Morton, now Secretary of Agriculture in Mr. Cleveland's Cabinet, who invented 'Arbor Day' and had it legalized as a holiday ; and we, with many other States, have followed the example thus set us. The custom of tree-planting is not, however, new, for the Germans have a commendable habit, as one writer tells us, of each member of a family living in the rural districts planting a tree at Wissuntide, which comes forty days after Easter. The old Mexican Indians also plant trees on certain days of the year when the moon is full, and name them after their children ; and the Aztecs used to plant a tree every time a child was born, and it bore the name of the child.

" Let us then take renewed interest in this day, and in the beautiful custom of planting memorial trees, remembering that at about the same time many, many others with us are endeavouring to repair the beauty of our land, to atone for the ravages which civilization has made.

"Wishing you a very happy springtime, and trusting that this year you may acquire a broader and deeper interest in trees and tree culture,

" I am,

" Yours very cordially,

"J. F. CROOKER,

" Superintendent."

### Freedom of Behaviour.

. Freedom of behaviour exists in all classes in America, and seemed to me to be specially marked in the schools, whether day schools or Sunday schools. Children in ragged clothes and without shoes went to work at the blackboard before the class with apparently perfect unconcern. The freedom with which the children engaged in " busy work " moved about the room, whilst the teacher was engaged in teaching the rest of the form, was striking, and at first sight seemed to imply lack of discipline or order ; but, since this freedom of behaviour is accompanied by admirable order and discipline whenever general orders are given—for the Americans have strong reverence for forms of law—the lack of discipline was apparent only, for it is clear that such freedom could exist only where the highest kind of discipline was exercised.

This national freedom has its drawbacks, for, entering as it does into the State laws, it is found that no reforms can go faster than those to which the people are educated.

### *Co-education.*

The Grade Schools (Primary and Grammar) contain the bulk of the girls and boys of the country, and in these schools boys and girls have, with the exception of manual work, such as cooking, sewing, and metal working, the same curriculum ; for it is held that girls and boys require the same backbone of study, since, whatever their work, they need equal readiness in using their powers.

In the High Schools also, though at certain points

subjects are elective and optional, the courses of study for boys and girls are in the main the same. Co-education, though now so largely practised, is of comparatively recent date. Some fifty or sixty years ago, the children who now attend the Primary Schools attended dame schools or private schools, while separate schools for boys and girls in the grammar grades was the universal rule.

When the Public Schools were established, the present condition of things came as the result of development.

In Chicago, co-education is universal, except in the Manual Training Schools. West of Chicago, I came across no exception to it. In St. Louis separate education was first tried, but had to give way to co-education. In Indianapolis co-education is adopted from the lowest primary grade up to and including the State University. In the eastern cities the arrangements of the present day often depend largely on school tradition. In Pennsylvania co-education is common in the State, but not in the older cities, where, in places, a strong prejudice exists against it, though in the Primary Schools and in the Grammar Schools there is a strong tendency towards it. The Pratt Institute in Brooklyn is co-educational throughout, and co-education is strongly supported by the authorities. They say men become more tolerant and appreciative through it, and they claim it is good mentally, morally, and intellectually.

East Boston and all suburban districts of Boston have mixed schools, in which boys and girls work together. In the Primary Schools at Boston, co-education is universal with two or three inconsiderable exceptions, and these only in the lowest districts, and for the convenience of separating the backward scholars, mostly the children of poor immigrants who swarm into the country. In the Boston Grammar Schools there is every condition of co-education—*i.e.*, there are separate buildings, separate rooms in the same building, separate sides of the same room, and indiscriminate sitting. By the Massachusetts law, the graduating class, or highest class in the High School, is mixed, but in Boston there is one exception even to this.

I was told and could see that the girls of a High School, when educated with boys, have more dignity, quietness, and self-possession of manner than those who are educated with girls only; while boys, from mixing with girls, show the influence of wholesome restraint in their manners; otherwise girls and boys do not seem to have much marked influence on each other during school years. One lady remarked that as a girl she took no notice of boys, except of those above her in age and attainments, though another remarked that she was not sure that the apparent indifference was anything more than superficial.

By one authority not wholly in sympathy with co-education it was said that best results might follow co-education in the hands of a strong teacher, but worst results in the hands of a weak teacher ; but with one exception—that of a first year's class in a High School under a master—I was much struck with the bearing of the American school girl as being much more self-reliant than that of the English school girl.

Dr. Harris, Commissioner of Education in Washington D.C., when superintendent of the schools in St. Louis in 1870, makes the following quotation from Richter's "Levana" in his Report of that year :—

" To ensure modesty I would advise the education of the sexes together; for two boys will preserve twelve girls, or two girls twelve boys, innocent, amidst winks, jokes, and improprieties, merely by that instinctive sense which is the forerunner of natural modesty. But I will guarantee nothing in a school where girls are alone together, and still less where boys are."

Co-education is not restricted to the schools. Ann Arbor was the first Co-educational Institute for adults in America; but now State Universities are frequently co-educational, particularly in the West. And here I may mention a fact curious to an English mind, of the way in which women work with men, side by side in the same room, in all sorts of offices, whether of school superintendents, librarians, Boards of Education, or purely business or mercantile; and I was told that girls frequently act as draughtsmen in architects' offices. All this probably is due to the way in which the education of girls as well as of boys is claimed as a right, from which belief, indeed, co-education may be said to have sprung.

After having seen the results of co-education in America, and having heard it spoken of by those who are not only daily proving its effects, but also have themselves been subject to its influence, I feel that we, as a nation, are losing greatly by the way in which we almost persistently keep our boys and girls apart; hence, as Dr. Harris in this same Report sums up the advantages which belongs to co-education, I venture to quote largely from him. He points out:

I. "That economy is secured because co-education permits of better classification and larger classes."

II. "Discipline has improved continually, not only on the part of the boys, but on that of the girls as well."

" The rudeness and *abandon* which prevail among boys when separate at once give place to self-restraint in the presence of girls. The prurient sentimentality engendered by educating girls apart from boys, and manifested by a frivolous and silly bearing when such girls are brought into the society of the opposite sex, disappears almost entirely in mixed schools. In its place a quiet self-possession reigns. The consequence of this is a general prevalence of milder forms of discipline. Boys and girls originating—according to Nature's plan—in the same family as brother and sister, their culture should be together, so that the social instincts may be saved from abnormal diseased action. The natural dependence of each individual upon all the rest in society should not be prevented by isolating one sex from another during the most formative stages of growth."

III. Instruction is also greatly improved. "We find girls making wonderful advances even in mathematical studies, while boys seem to take hold of literature far better for the influence of the female portion of the class."

IV. "Individual development is far more sound and healthy. It has been found that schools kept exclusively for girls or boys require a much more strict surveillance on the part of the teacher. The girls, confined by themselves, develop the sexual tension much earlier, their imagination being the reigning faculty, and not bridled by intercourse with society in its normal form. So it is with boys, on the other hand. Daily association in the class-room prevents this tension, and supplies its place by indifference. Each sex testing its strength with the other on an intellectual plane in the presence of the teacher, each one seeing the weakness and strength of the other, learns to esteem what is essential at its true value. Sudden likes and dislikes, capricious fancies and romantic ideals give way for sober judgments not easily deceived by mere externals. This is the basis of that quiet self-possession before alluded to, and it forms the most striking mark of difference between the girls or boys educated in mixed schools and those educated in schools exclusively for one sex."

"That sexual tension be developed as late as possible and that all early love affairs be avoided is the desideratum, and experience has shown that association of the sexes on the plane of intellectual contest is the safest course to secure this end."

### *Foreign Element in Schools.*

A serious and disturbing element which has to be taken into account in the American schools is the great immigration that is always going on, particularly in the sea-board cities, as Boston and New York; the immigrants are mainly from the slums of Europe, among the worst being the Italians, the Russian Jews, the Poles, Hungarians, Portuguese, and Irish. The poorest immigrants remain in the first city to which they come, and create or swell slum districts, while the better class of immigrants push on into the interior. In Omaha, for instance, there are German, Bohemian, Swedish, Polish, and Danish settlements.

The settlers rapidly assimilate the American

ways, and though the new comers at first build and live in the ways of their fatherland, the children become Americans, which no doubt is due mainly to the fact that they are educated at the free schools of the nation.

At present it is felt that the schools are humanizing the immigrant population, and improving them for the next generation; though the fear is not absent that the rapidity with which immigration is going on will swamp the native American element.

### *Compulsory Education.*

Compulsory Education, though existing in some States, is by no means universal.

I did not inquire about this in all the places I visited, but found it did not exist in Omaha, Indianapolis, District of Columbia, nor in Pennsylvania, though in the latter place there is a growing sentiment that it should be made so in consequence of the large influx of foreigners.

In Omaha, although there is no Compulsory Education, children who do not attend schools are looked after by charitable organizations.

In Boston a yearly census is taken of the children and the schools they attend. If a child does not attend any school, the cause of his absence is inquired into, and the parent is fined for the non-attendance of his child at school. The Truant Officers frequently find cases of distress, and thus become the agents for charitable people.

By the Massachusetts State law, the private schools must be as good as the public schools. The method of proving is to lay a suit against the parent, who at once appeals to the private school, so that the onus of proof falls on the school.

### Teachers and Teaching.

One superintendent remarked to me that the American teachers are ambitious and enthusiastic.

There is very little prefunctory treatment of work. The teaching is live teaching.

Teachers in District Schools under township Committees show the same energy. Work is done in all branches with almost savage industry and ferocious energy, although done not unfrequently by those who have no intention of making teaching a profession, for many young men go in for teaching first so as to earn and save money for fitting themselves for other work, or to raise capital to go into other and more lucrative employments. This strong characteristic of energy, which tends to produce intense nervousness, is doubtless the outcome of the history of the nation.

There is no leisure class in America. A man of leisure is considered more or less a "loafer." The position which women hold there is far above that accorded to them in the "Old Country," and is, I cannot but think, a source of strength to the nation.

They came into power at the time of the war. It was necessary for them to take the place and conduct the business of the fighting men. Under the emergency they proved themselves to be possessed of powers with which they had not previously been credited, and the standing they then secured has never been resigned.

In some cities men and women teachers are paid on the same scale, but this is by no means a universal rule; and since men can usually earn better incomes than by teaching, while women cannot, the supply of male teachers is not equal to the demand, and the supply of females is in excess; for instance, in Philadelphia out of 2,900 teachers, 100 were men and 2,800 women.

In Boston, in 1892, the regular teachers numbered 1345; of these 158 were males, 1187 females, while in the same city the special teachers for Evening Classes and such subjects as drawing and physical exercises numbered 269; of these 112 were males, 157 females. The positions most frequently secured by men are those of Superintendents and Principals of Schools, though they, not unfrequently, work with women in the High Schools; for it must be remembered that women teach mixed classes of boys and girls in the High Schools, where the students often are from 18 to 20 years of age.

## *Appointment of Teachers.*

The appointment of teachers is governed by local laws, and as the details as to their appointments and qualifications have probably as many variations as there are States and Cities, it will be impossible to do more than point out general resemblances, and then cite particular instances.

One point to which I would call special attention is the fact that nowhere did I find an instance of any one being allowed to teach unless he or she had passed some test which was accepted by the appointing Board. These tests vary greatly. In the District Schools they usually take the form of Examinations held at regular intervals by the

County Superintendent under the State Superintendent.

As an instance, I quote from " The School Law of the State of Colorado," the arrangements laid down there being similar to those in many of the other States.

" On the last Friday of February, May, August, and November in each year, he (the County Superintendent) shall meet all persons desirous of passing an examination as teachers, in some suitable room at the county seat, notice of which shall be given in some newspaper in the county, or in case there is no paper published in the county, he shall give such notice as may by him be deemed necessary; at which time he shall examine all such applicants in orthography, reading, writing, English grammar, geography, the history of the United States, physiology, the laws of health, the elements of the natural sciences, theory and practice of teaching, and the school law of the State." (See Section 15.)

" If the applicant is to teach in a school of high grade, the examination shall extend to such additional branches of study as are to be pursued in such school. If satisfied of the competency to teach, and of the good moral character of the applicant, he (the County Superintendent) shall give such applicant a certificate as provided in the following section, but he shall not issue a certificate, except a temporary one, except the applicant be examined at the regular quarterly examination." (See Section 15.)

" The certificates issued by the County Superintendent shall be of three grades, distinguished as first, second, and third. The first grade certificate shall be valid for two years; the second grade for one year; the third grade for six months." (See Section 16.)

" The superintendent shall keep an official record, in a suitable book, of the persons so examined, containing the name, age, nationality, date of examination, and grade of certificate issued; he shall also retain for six months the written answers of all applicants at the regular examinations, and hold the same subject to the order of the State Board of Education." (See Section 16.)

" No District Board shall employ any person to teach in any of the public schools of the State unless such person shall have a license to teach, issued from the proper district, county, or State authority, and in full force at the date of employment ; and any teacher who shall commence teaching in any such school without such license shall forfeit all claim to compensation out of the school fund for the term so teaching without license." (See Section 60.)

This granting of temporary certificates acts as a strong inducement to an ambitious teacher to carry on private study side by side with the teaching done, with the hope of securing a certificate of a higher grade than that already held. To give facilities for this study, Normal Institutes are held in some States. These Institutes differ from Normal Schools in that they are held during the long vacation, for the purpose of helping those teachers who are unable to take a full course at a Normal School.

In addition to the certificates granted by the County Superintendent, some States grant State diplomas, and I again quote from " The School Law of the State of Colorado " :—

" The State Board of Education is hereby authorized to grant State diplomas to such teachers as may be found to possess the requisite scholarship and culture, and who may also exhibit satisfactory evidence of an unexceptionable moral character, and whose eminent professional ability has been established by not less than two years' successful teaching in the Public Schools of this State.

"Such diplomas shall supersede the necessity of any and all other examinations of persons holding the same by county, city, or local examiners, and shall be valid in any county, city, town, or district in the State, unless revoked by the State Board of Education" (Section 3).

The tests which are imposed on teachers in cities are regulated mainly by Boards of Education.

In some cases the Board will accept State certificates, either of a Normal School or of a University, or any other recognised certificate. In other cases they require the candidates to pass special Examinations held under the Superintendent of the City; in one city where appointments of teachers are made by examination only, the examinees are not allowed even to write their names on their Examination papers.

No one can teach in a Public School in Boston who has not either been through the Normal School or passed successfully the Supervisors' examination, for which one year's experience in teaching is essential. They are then appointed temporarily for one year, confirmed for three years, after which they are appointed permanently on good behaviour.

In another city teachers were required rapidly, because the Schools grew suddenly ; hence High School graduates were appointed who had not gone through Normal training. At first the Principals of the Schools reported that the work of the High School graduates was as satisfactory as that of the Normal students ; but after a time the marks given by the Principals to the Normal students and High School graduates for teaching and disciplining were, as a rule, in the ratio of two to one.

Some hold that the training of teachers can be done as well by Principals as by Normal Schools ; as an illustration of this, in Chicago the " cadet " system is followed. Cadets watch work for some months, acting as substitutes when such are needed, and when appointed as teachers begin with the lowest grade.

Teachers coming to Chicago from the outside have only to pass the specified Examination, and when once appointed, their position is fairly permanent. There are in this city between 3,000 and 4,000 teachers ; of these only 100 to 200 drop out annually, and that mostly either by death or marriage.

In the District of Columbia three Commissioners are appointed by Congress ; these appoint Trustees, who appoint teachers. The Trustees are guided in their opinion by the Superintendent, who in turn is guided by the Supervising Principals. Teachers here must have a Normal School certificate, or must pass the Examination set by the Supervisors. Graduates of the High School must pass through the Normal School before they can be appointed as teachers in the Grade Schools.

The plan of educating teachers in a Normal School attached to a High School is frequently followed, and struck me as likely to be an element of future weakness, though I was told that if the Normal School was good, the fact that the whole education of the teacher had been carried on in the same place was an element of strength.

### Boards of Education.

The importance which attaches to Boards of Education in America makes me feel that I cannot omit all mention of them.

The Board forms the governing body of the

Schools within a given area, and the Superintendent of the Schools is the executive officer of the Board.

All classes of people may be found on these Boards, and they are appointed or elected in various ways; the following are a few instances.

The Board of Education in Boston consists of twenty-four members, elected by voters to hold office for three years.

In New York, in Brooklyn, and in Chicago, the Mayor nominates the members of the Board of Education, and there was some talk of this plan being adopted in Boston.

In Philadelphia the Board is composed of one member from each of the thirty-six sections into which the city is divided. These members are appointed by the Common Pleas judges; two women are on this Board.

The Omaha Board of Education consists of fifteen members, about half of whom retire yearly. All these are voted for " at large."

In Indianapolis there are eleven members, who are elected by the people; these, while taking charge of the School finances, practically leave the course of study to the Superintendent — a good arrangement, but only rarely seen.

The School districts in Indianapolis do not coincide with political districts; this is intentional, in order to diminish possibilities of political interference. So far this has been fairly well secured, and it is hoped that it may continue so.

In Denver the Board of Education consists of six members. Two are elected annually, and that when no other elections are taking place; hence no politics have been introduced into the School management.

Washington, District of Columbia, has one Superintendent, one lady assistant, and eight Supervisors, each having a special district to supervise. The Superintendent is appointed by three Commissioners, and the finances are managed by six Trustees. The Superintendent, the Supervisors, and the Trustees, all visit the Schools. These visits are recorded, and are reported by the Principals of the Schools in their monthly reports.

These instances show some of the various ways in which the Boards are appointed, and will, to a large extent, explain the somewhat curious phenomena occasionally met with, in reference especially to teachers. In one city, a Board suddenly decreed that every teacher in that city, whatever his or her standing, should pass a fresh and rather comprehensive examination, in order to retain his or her position! And when the Schools are governed by a number of men who may or may not know anything of education, the results must necessarily be somewhat uncertain, and the position of a Superintendent very difficult. One important part of his work then becomes that of educating his Board!

### School Buildings.

In the High Schools there is usually a large hall, somewhat square in general form, well arranged with seats; but I remember no instance of a Grade School having such an assembly hall.

The school-rooms are large and well lighted, but kept at a very high temperature, 68° to 70° Fahr. being considered the desirable temperature. In one school I visited, the children were being dismissed because, the heating apparatus being out of order, the temperature could not be raised above 56°, and it was " not safe for children to sit in such cold! "

In most—perhaps all—cities, all the Public Schools are connected by telephone with the Superintendent's office.

The dressing-room accommodation appeared to me insufficient.

No school in Brooklyn had separate rooms for dressing-rooms ; the arrangements made were various. In one school presses were in the large corridors ; in another the blackboards were fixed on sliding-doors, which hid recesses where the hats and cloaks were hung.

The money expended on these buildings is often very large. Not infrequently, especially with District Schools in country places, the only building not of wood will be the school-house.

In travelling across the prairies, or high up on the Rocky Mountains, occasionally a good substantial building may be seen, contrasting strangely with the little shanties or log huts of the settlers. If the traveller should inquire about one of these substantial-looking buildings, the answer is invariable—" That is a school-house."

Nowhere do Americans seem to grudge money for schools. In Denver the cost of the High School, which has a magnificent entrance hall, was $325,000. The total cost of fifteen school buildings in the same city to May 5th, 1890, was $819,861, or an average cost per building of over £10,000 ! These Schools struck me as being the best school buildings I saw anywhere. The corridors were wide, the staircases in central positions, the rooms lofty and of good area, the desks arranged so as to leave abundance of space by the blackboards, which go all round the rooms, as well as good aisles between each row of desks. Each class-room had three doors : one for general entrance, one leading to girls' dressing-room, one leading to boys' dressing-room. But although the buildings were so good, the amount of playground was small, and this latter I found to be the case in most places.

### *Courses of Study.*

I was very anxious when first starting on my tour to America to see whether or not the way in which courses of study were planned for all the Schools of a city produced lack of individuality and crushed out originality, or whether it was a source of strength.

Speaking generally, the impression I received was not only that originality and individuality were allowed full play when they were good, but that the course of study, followed up as it is with frequent supervision, proved a great corrective of the mistakes which so often take place in the hands of a weak teacher.

In Boston the Board of Education aims at making a man feel responsible, and yet feel that he belongs to a system; they therefore leave all liberty consistent with order to the discretion of the teacher, and, as a consequence, intense individuality is noticeable everywhere in Boston.

Mr. Powell, Superintendent of the Washington Schools, told me that great freedom is allowed to the teacher, as much freedom as is consistent with having a system.

The same sentiments were expressed by the Superintendents both of Indianapolis and of Omaha, and, while I have mentioned special instances, the same, no doubt, might be said of many other cities.

In some places teachers have the right of claiming a day for visiting other schools; in one city one day per annum is granted; in another city one day per term is not only granted, but must be so used, and a report of the visits made and of the lessons heard has to be sent in to the Superintendent.

In addition to this, the Superintendent may send a teacher to visit a Grade at any time.

Teachers fully appreciate these advantages; in

D

one instance I met a teacher who, while her class for some special reason was having a holiday, was utilizing her time in visiting another class of the same grade.

The fact that the same course of study has to be followed in every school in a city gives to this visiting a double advantage ; for a teacher can observe not only general methods of teaching, but also how, in another person's hands, the same work in which she is engaged assumes quite a different form.

In Boston the Principals of schools, within broad limits, organize their own schools. This condition I found prevailing largely in the schools of the various towns I visited, but in different degrees ; and where fully carried out, the schools struck me as being healthier, and freer from unnatural constraint, amongst both teachers and taught.

No one will, I think, deny that the tone of the teaching staff is an index to the tone of the scholars, and I found that where the Superintendent attempted to command in detail, as well as in general guiding principles, the teacher lost the freshness and vigour of work which comes from the need of exercising one's own sense of responsibility, and the Superintendent, in visiting the various rooms, was received not so much as a friend who would give encouragement, help, and advice, but as a taskmaster whose presence was rather to be dreaded.

One great difference which struck me as existing between the courses of study for the primary grades and the usual curriculum for pupils of a similar age in our own secondary schools was in the number of subjects taught.

I give two instances, one taken from an Eastern, one from a Western school.

The subjects laid down in the course of study of the Boston Primary Schools, Class II., are :—

Moral training ... ... ½ hour per week.
Physical training ... ... 1½ hours „
Observation lessons and manual
   training ... ... ... 3 „ „
Drawing ... ... ... 1½ „ „
Singing ... ... ... ... 1 hour „
Language (this includes oral
   and written exercises, read
   ing, and writing) ... ... 11½ hours „
Arithmetic ... ... ... 3½ „ „

In Chicago the course of study laid down for the first year or grade consists of :—

Language (this includes oral
  work, reading, writing, spell-
    ing), arithmetic, singing ...   1¼ hours per week.
Form study and colour drawing   1¼  ,,     ,,
Miscellaneous (this includes personal habits, conduct, physical
  culture, sewing).

In Chicago the course of study is revised annually. Not much is changed in the regular subjects, as arithmetic, reading, and grammar, but subjects taught in the grammar grades, such as science and geography, are subject to revision.

As a general rule the study of languages and of mathematics is deferred until the pupils enter the high schools. Indeed, one striking point in nearly all the graded schools of the country is the absence of foreign languages in the school curriculum.

The fact that by far the greater portion of the continent is English-speaking removes the incentive to the study of foreign languages which exists in England.

In high schools generally Greek, Latin, and modern languages are taught, and the pupils may by choice take two or three languages, according to the special regulations of the place.

In St. Loüis there is a large German element, and to a certain extent German was at one time studied by the younger children, and became the medium of instruction in the Public Schools. This continued for about twenty years, when there arose against the practice a strong native American feeling, and it was determined to sweep German out of the Primary Schools; this was done in St. Louis, and in other cities to the west and south of St. Louis.

In some manufacturing towns, as Lawrence and Holyoke, there is a large French-Canadian population, where Jesuitical schools attempted to keep their hold over the population by using French. A law was, however, made that if parents sent their children to any school where the medium of instruction was other than English the parents should be fined. Consequently the usage of French was abolished, since the Jesuits, in order to retain their pupils, adopted the English language.

One small but important point of difference in management between a grade or class in America and a form or class in a secondary school in England is the time given to private work in school hours.

A grade under one teacher is usually divided into

two classes, and, while the teacher is hearing or teaching one class, the other is doing " busy work " or preparation.

Even in the high schools each pupil usually has one or more divisions in which to prepare work.

I now give some detailed account of work done in certain subjects, as I feel that an examination of parts of the " courses of study " will perhaps be one of the best ways of estimating the kind of work that is being carried on in the Graded Schools of America.

### Arithmetic.

I wish to call attention particularly to the teaching of arithmetic in the primary grades, as the method is very different from ours, and has many advantages.

Usually the first year's work is the " teaching numbers from 1 to 10; this involves the teaching of the processes of addition, subtraction, multiplication, and division (objectively) with these numbers and their parts. The number of problems required to do the work thoroughly would fill from 300 to 350 pages of an arithmetic book " (Springfield, Mass., Syllabus of Work).

Addition, subtraction, and division tables are taught with the multiplication tables; and no example is given in addition or in multiplication which involves the adding of any figures not learnt. Thus in a first grade, where all tables of 2's are learnt, the addition sum would be somewhat as follows:—$2+2+1+2+2+1+1+1+2+2$; and not until a child knows the addition table of 3's as well as the multiplication, division, and subtraction of 3's, are 3's used in an addition sum.

All number is taught objectively, the children making problems for themselves from pictures and stones. "Every new thought process in arithmetic must be developed at first objectively in any grade," as, for example, square root and cube root in the seventh and eighth grades, as well as work in the primary grades.

In some schools, as in Springfield, Mass., and in Denver, Colorado, elementary fractions are taught in the first grade, where no number higher than 10 is used. The children learn (objectively) $\frac{1}{2}$, $\frac{1}{4}$, $\frac{1}{3}$, and use them in connection with any number to 10; while in the second grade, where the numbers to be mastered are from 10 to 20, the fractions taught (objectively) are $\frac{1}{2}$, $\frac{1}{4}$, $\frac{1}{8}$, $\frac{1}{3}$, $\frac{1}{6}$, $\frac{1}{5}$, $\frac{1}{7}$.

In concluding this subject, I should like again to quote from the Springfield Syllabus of Work

" Nearly all topics in arithmetic are simple in their elements, but difficult in their advanced development. Hence it is a mistake in grading the work in a course of study to assume that one topic is to be 'finished' before another is begun. On the contrary, the elements of many topics should be begun in the lower grades, and then the work in each be made more and more difficult through the various grades until it is finished."

### *Geography.*

While at Indianapolis I spent a whole day in hearing the teaching of geography in the successive grades, and was very much indebted to Miss Cropsey, the Assistant Superintendent, for her kindness in arranging this plan for me.

I found the teaching most intelligent, and the children most interested.

I now give the directions as to the teaching of geography extracted from the course of study in the Manual of the Public Schools of Indianapolis for 1892–93, as it shows the care with which any particular study can be, and I find frequently is, thought out in detail. In doing this, I also give the work under " Reading " in the first two grades, since this shows the way in which the elements of geography are taught.

## Grade I. B.

Reading conversation lessons, based mainly upon the study of nature—plants and animals. The instructions in reading and number should be closely connected with the instruction in form and colour and the observation of nature. (See Syllabus on Observation Lessons, and general remarks under Language, Grade II. B.)

The sand table may be used in illustrating reading and number stories, and the children should be encouraged to represent their ideas of hills, valleys, streets, trees, parks, ponds, brooks.

## Grade I. A.

Supplementary reading should be based upon the study of nature and appropriate literature, which gives the relation of the child to nature, also the literature which brings the child into true relations with humanity, the family, the school, society, and the nation. "Little People of Other Lands" read to the children.

Plants, animals, and minerals should be studied; and pupils should be led to notice the phenomena of each season.

### Grade II. B.

Language—composition. Oral in connection with lessons upon plants and animals.

In presenting this work, it is best to give, first, the poetic view, giving the life and habits of the plant or the animal in its natural environment and its relation to man ; second, the structure adapted to the life of the individual, as "The root takes up food for the plant," and at the same time to give the relative position of parts; third, a careful description of parts with reference to form, size, and colour, and other qualities given to the intelligence through the senses.

This work should lead to a view of the unity of each living thing in itself and its necessary connection with other things. It should also lead to habits of close observation, and to independent and honest statement of facts. (All of this work should employ the child's knowledge of colour and form in illustration of the subject.)

Geography. All study of form, colour, plants, or animals ; all observations upon the weather or upon the phenomena of the changing seasons ; all stories of children of other lands, are contributions to the study of geography. The observations made by each school upon the changes of season should be recorded in some convenient way, and children should often turn back and compare with the present phenomena. " Seven Little Sisters " read to the children.

## GRADE II. A.

Geography. (See Grade II. B.) Study a few of the typical forms of land and water, as children have opportunities to observe them, as hill, valley, river, pond. Use the sand table; pictures can be used to help make clear and permanent the concepts based upon observation. Study water, as dew, rain, hail, snow, ice, steam. " Robinson Crusoe " read to children.

## GRADE III. B.

Geography. Continue work begun in previous grades. Children should keep their own record of the weather and of the phenomena of the seasons. Note that the sun appears to move.

Read "Seven Little Sisters." Show the picture of the earth as given in that book. Learn poetic descriptions of the earth as a whole (" Great, wide, wonderful, beautiful world "). Use the pictures and descriptions of the School Reader to aid in making permanent concepts gained elsewhere; Appleton's Third : " By the Brook," " The White Bear," " The Mountain," " Lost in a Balloon," " Caught by the Tide," " The River," " North Wind."

Teach points of the compass. Draw the map of the schoolroom, for the purpose of teaching the idea and use of a map.

### Grade III. A.

Geography. Size and shape of the earth. (Story of " Long Ago " in Appleton's Third Reader.) The shape of the horizon on the water or on a plain. What seems to be the shape of the sky? Forms of land and water, with water flowing over the land (Frye's " Child in Nature," p. 82). Teach by observation if possible. Lessons from King's Geographical Readers. Water flowing through the soil, and soil-making (Frye, pp. 82–88). Read with the children " Brooks and Brook-basins," also lessons from King's Geographical Readers. Air by experience; water in the air (Frye, pp. 89, 83). Stories of races and religions, occupations and commerce (Frye, pp. 118–120). Read " Aunt Martha's Corner Cupboard."

Model and draw map of the school yard and school district. Show map of the city, and note the relation of the district to the city. Locate the principal streets and public buildings. Occupations of people at home, what they do for a living; means of communication with other places; laws of the city, and who make them.

## GRADE IV. B.

Geography. Elementary Geography, Indiana Series.

### I. *The Earth as a Whole.*

1. Teach form, size, motions, and position as to the rays of the sun, as a basis for the explanation of the general distribution of heat over the surface of the earth (Lessons VI., XII., and XIII.).

2. From the foregoing lead the pupil to infer that the hottest parts of the surface of the earth are near the equator, and that as the distance from the equator increases the heat diminishes (Lesson XIV.).

3. Teach the general distribution of plants and animals, and lead the pupil to see that it depends upon the general distribution of heat (Lessons XV. and XVI.).

4. Teach that the surface of the earth consists of land and water; that the large bodies of land are called continents; and that the large bodies of

water are called oceans, and all the oceans together are called " the sea" (Lesson VII.).

5. Teach that some parts of the land rise higher above the level of the sea than others; that as we ascend high mountains we see that the temperature grows cooler until we find ice and snow. This will introduce the fact that elevation modifies the general distribution of heat. Lead the children to infer the kinds of plants and animals that are found on high elevations (Lesson IX.).

6. Minerals. Teach where they are found. Mention the common ones. Lead the pupil to see how useful they are to man, and that he is likely to try to discover where he can get them with the least trouble and expense (Lesson XVII.).

7. Refer to the fact that people must have food, clothes, houses, etc., to make them comfortable; that these cannot be obtained without work, and so we find people working to procure these things (Lesson XVIII.).

8. Lead the pupil to get an idea of government by referring to rules in games and school. See directions in preceding grades. Tell the pupils about the different kinds of government (Lesson XIX.).

9. Read stories or descriptions that bear on any part of the geography work of this grade.

10. Read stories of the different races of men in the world (Lesson XX.).

II. Parts of the Earth.

1. Home observations.

(1) Have pupils note the apparent motions of the sun, with results of same (Frye, p. 94.).

(2) Observe habits of plants and animals in the different seasons (Frye, pp. 102 and 106).

(3) The common minerals found in our own locality or state.

(4) The occupation of the people.

(5) Current events that have relation to the geography study of the grade.

2. North America.

(1) Its position as to the direct rays of the sun and as to the oceans that touch it.

(2) Its general outline.

(3) A general idea of its size.

(4) Its chief elevations.

(5) Its chief rivers and lakes.

(6) Its climate, plants, and animals.

(7) Its principal minerals, and where found (in general Lessons XXII. and XXIII.).

3. South America studied by the same general plan as North America (Lessons XXVII. and XXVIII.).

4. The United States.

(1) Position.

(2) Size.

(3) Outline form.

(4) Chief elevations, slopes, rivers, and lakes.

(5) Chief plants, animals, and minerals.

(6) The people: their chief occupations (Lessons XXIII. and L.).   (See map on p. 68.)

### GRADE IV. A.

Geography.    Elementary Geography, Indiana Series.

### I. *The Earth as a Whole.*

1. Review form, size, position, and motions of the earth as taught in IV. B.

2. Show that the general distribution of heat determines the general direction of the winds.    Tell about the trade winds.

3. Current events that bear on any work outlined in this or the preceding grade.

### II. *Parts of the Earth.*

1. Review North America in order to teach the

physical features of the Dominion of Canada, Greenland, Alaska, Mexico, and Central America (Lessons **XXIV.** to **XXVI.**).

2. Study Europe and Asia in outline, and then more in detail as separate continents. (See Parker's " How to Study Geography," pp. 42–47.) Study these continents by a plan similar to the one given for North America in IV. B (Lessons **XXX.** and **XXXVI.**).

3. Study the following countries :—
   (1) Europe,—
      (*a*) British Isles (Lesson **XXXI.**).
      (*b*) Germany (Lesson **XXXIII.**).
      (*c*) Russia (Lesson **XXXII.**).
      (*d*) France and Switzerland (Lesson **XXXIX.**).
      (*e*) Spain (Lesson **XXXV.**).
   (2) Asia,—
      (*a*) China (Lesson **XXXVIII.**).
      (*b*) Japan and Indo-China (Lesson **XXXIX.**).
      (*c*) British India (Lesson **XL.**).

## Grade V. B.

Geography.    Elementary Geography, Indiana Series.

**E**

I. *The Earth as a Whole.*

1. Review IV. B and IV. A, and teach that the rotation of the earth modifies the direction of the winds.

2. Lead the pupils to see the earth as a great ball, whose surface is composed of land and water; and that the land is made up chiefly of the continents studied; also that the water or sea is made up of the different oceans (Lessons XLVII. and XLVIII.).

3. Compare the general structure of the land masses. (See Parker.)

II. *Parts of the Earth.*

1. Africa as North America in IV. B. Make the work on the countries very light (Lessons XLII. to XLIV.).

2. Oceania as given in the book (Lessons XLV. and XLVI.).

3. United States by groups as given in the book (Lessons LI. to LXII. inclusive).

## Grade V. A.

Geography. Complete Geography, I n d i a n a Series.

I. *The Earth as a Whole.*

(1) Mathematical geography.

1. Form, size, position, and motions of the earth, as determining the general distribution of the heat and winds (pp. 3, 5, and 7).

(2) Physical geography.

1. Teach general direction of winds (p. 36) and ocean currents (p. 35) as determined by general distribution of heat.

2. Special distribution of heat, direction of ocean currents and winds, as determined by elevation, slope, and relative position of land and water bodies (see Parker, pp. 52–54) (pp. 12, 13, and 14).

3. Distribution of rain fall and soil as determined by the preceding.

4. Distribution of plants (pp. 43–52).

5. Distribution of animals ( pp. 53–63).

6. Distribution of minerals.

GRADE VI. B.

Geography.   Complete Geography, Indiana Series.

I.   *The Earth as a Whole.*

(*a*) Mathematical geography.

1. Review V. A.

2. Study " change of season " more thoroughly than in V. A.

(*b*) Physical geography.

1. Review ocean currents and winds and rainfall carefully, noting their effect upon the climate of a country (pp. 33, 36, and 43).

2. Draw belts showing the general distribution of plants and animals.

(*c*) Political.

1. Distribution of occupations and productions (pp. 61–63)

2. Distribution of races ( p. 61).

3. Distribution of governments ( p. 64).

4. Distribution of religions ( p. 64).

5. Commerce. Show that it depends upon the physical conditions of a country (p. 130). Show how it is carried on between countries and between different parts of the same country.

### Grade VI. A.

Geography. Complete Geography, Indiana Series.

### I. *The Earth as a Whole.*

Political geography.

1. Distribution of political divisions and governments.

2. In what belts are the principal cities of the world? Learn what each is noted for.

## II. *Parts of the Earth.*

1. Special study of the United States ( pp. 68–89).

(*a*) Mathematical.

(*b*) Physical.

(*c*) Political.

2. Special study of Indiana by the same plan.

### GRADE VII. B.

Geography. Complete Geography. Indiana Series.

## I. *The Earth as a Whole.*

(*a*) Mathematical.

Review what has been learned in order to show that it is the basis of the physical conditions upon the earth, because it determines the general distribution of heat and moisture.

(*b*) Physical.

1. Review, showing that the divisions of land and water and the elevation of land determine the special distribution of heat and moisture, and that out of this grows the distribution of plants and animals.

2. The distribution of plants, animals, and minerals determines the distribution of occupations of the people.

3. Study the continents enough to enable the pupil to see that the general truths learned apply to the individual continents.

4. Study the structure of the following countries that have figured in history: Persia and Syria, Egypt, Greece, Italy, Spain, France, Great Britain, Germany, Holland, and the United States. (See Parker.)

(c) Political.

1. Show all countries are related to one another, and how they all depend upon the mathematical and physical conditions of the earth.

2. Lead pupils from this to see that the earth seems intended for the house of man.

3. Study the political features of the countries named under " Physical " in this grade.

4. Distribution of nations (Parker, p. 388).

5. Distribution of races (Parker, p. 334).

NOTE.—" Political" is used in this course of study to include all human institutions.

In grades higher than VII. B I find the study of history as a subject is substituted for that of geography, though to the latter much attention is given in studying history.

# MANUAL, TECHNICAL, AND TECHNOLOGICAL TRAINING.

THE growing attention which is being paid to manual training in America must eventually have most marked results in the improvement of the nation as a whole, and of the artisans and mechanics in particular, as regards both intelligence and skill in handling materials of all kinds.

I found in Boston and also in Brooklyn that manual, technical, and technological training were regarded as three distinct kinds of training. Probably this distinction holds good generally, but the country is so large that I prefer to mention instances rather than to run the risk of making the mistakes which follow from generalising from a few particulars.

In the Pratt Institute in Brooklyn the schemes for manual and technical training are very comprehensive, and while classes for manual training are open to all, only trade students learn technical work ; and while learning they are not earning money, but are supported by parents or friends. Manual training is education given to develop powers of body, irrespective of the articles made ;

technical training is education given to prepare for mechanical arts; technological training is higher than technical training, inasmuch as it gives higher scientific study, and trains engineers and physicists.

The Pratt Institute was established in 1887, and was endowed by Mr. Pratt, senior.

The Drexel Institute in Philadelphia, more recently established, is, I understand, on the same lines.

I am unable to speak of the relative merits of these institutes; but having spent some time in the Pratt Institute, will base my remarks upon what I there saw.

It seemed to me most complete in organisation, arrangements, and appliances; no department, except that involving a purely literary course of study, being omitted. Co-education is believed in very strongly, mentally and morally, and is fully carried out.

A High School with a three years' course is attached to the Institute, and is attended by girls and boys. Evening classes are held on a variety of subjects, attendance at which is not restricted by sex or age; but the main part of the work is carried on in the Institute proper, which contains 13,000 students, of whom 9,000 are women or girls.

To enumerate all the classes would take too much space. Some parts of the course are compulsory, but others are elective. Opportunity is given — and naturally is used almost exclusively by girls—of learning, in rooms specially designed for the purpose, cookery, laundry, and needlework.

The cooking-room was most complete in its arrangements, and allowed no perfunctoriness in the teaching. All recipes had to be reduced or enlarged; *e.g.*, one tomato might be the quantity for each girl to cook, but the recipe might be given for a peck of tomatoes.

The same thoroughness was manifest in the laundry department.

Needlework included all its branches, as dressmaking, millinery, plain sewing, embroidery.

In the latter, original designing was greatly encouraged. In reference to designing I may add that, in addition to designs for embroidery, girls—boys too if they wish—design for carpets, cloths, silks, and silver; and their designs are not infrequently bought by New York and other merchants.

The architectural drawing class is frequently attended by girls, who act as draughtsmen in architects' offices. Miss Hayden, who was the architect of the Women's Building at Chicago, was a graduate of the Pratt Institute.

The Technological Institute in Boston was equally interesting; but I omit an account of it from my report, since the work I undertook had special reference to the Graded Schools.

I will close this part of my report by referring to the manual work I saw, which had more immediate reference to Graded Schools.

In the Schools at Philadelphia, which city ranks high for its manual training, I inspected a full course of sewing, the general plan of which was that each girl should at the beginning of a term make a "term piece," *i.e.*, a piece containing specimens of all new stitches to be done in the term. When this was completed, a garment might be brought from home on which to practise the new work learnt. Each term a review of all work learnt in previous terms was required.

Clay modelling is largely practised in Philadelphia, and in Washington, D.C.; in this boys, being less deft with their fingers than girls, require more practice of common things.

There are three kinds of clay modelling: scooping out the clay, so as to leave the form desired in a hollow in the slab; cutting away surroundings, so as to leave the form as if laid on the slab; building up the object desired with the hands and free from any slab.

Washington appeared to me very complete in its appliances for manual training. They have separate accommodation for cooking, for sewing, for carpenters, for turning lathes, and for working in metals; and as manual training is made compulsory for the last two years in the grammar grades and the first year in the High School, it is found that students generally wish to continue the training so soon as it becomes elective, and, consequently, very excellent results are seen.

In Indianapolis there is a Manual Training School in connection with the High School; but it chiefly, almost entirely, confines itself to working in wood. Some modelling in sand is done in the grades, also drawing and needlework, otherwise I did not find manual training taught in these grades.

I was told that St. Louis is good for its perfection of manual training, but this I had no opportunity of inspecting.

In Chicago a special Manual High School is established, which is distinct from the seven Classical High Schools, though ranking equal with them. It contains about 300 boys, no girls having at present applied, and gives training in carpentry, iron-foundry, and machinery work. A similar school, supported by private individuals, has been established for some of the Grammar Schools, and a few schools, mostly experimental, for the teaching of Slöjd.

In Boston, as examples of the way in which private individuals have helped and are helping in the cause of education, I should like to mention that one lady maintained a Cookery School at private cost, until success was assured, and the movement was adopted by the Board of Education, to whom she then handed over her school for the benefit of the city ; also a school for the teaching of Slöjd has been started by private enterprise, and one for the training of normal students in physical exercises, for the purpose of improving the physical exercises in the Graded Schools of the city.

*Drawing.*

In most schools considerable attention is paid to drawing all through the school career, from the earliest primary grade to the High School. The Prang Drawing Company, which has its head-quarters at Boston, has, I should judge, been the means of securing good work over a large area in the Schools of the United States.

As a short sketch of the principles and origin of the Prang system may be helpful in understanding the power which drawing has become in the American Schools, I give some extracts of the system taken from the pamphlets issued by the Company :—

" The system, which was originated by Walter Smith, was based on the South Kensington work, and derived its name from Mr. Prang, who, with Mr. Clarke, was publisher for Walter Smith. The course of instruction, as arranged by the Prang Education Company, covers eight years, or the time spent by a child in the primary and grammar grades ; but it does not stop there. It arranges for normal art classes, and for teaching by correspond-ence, and has now (1893) about 700 students in the normal classes."

The Company says :—

" The first organised effort to establish drawing
as a fundamental study in the Public Schools was
made in Massachusetts in 1870. Ever since that
time the movement for art education has been
increasing in strength and influence. The kinder-
garten movement, the movement for manual training, and that for art education stand, in fact, for
three great educational forces, which are re-shaping
the whole system of instruction in our public schools.
These three great forces, working in unison, have
helped to bring about a radical change in the
character of school instruction in drawing.

" This study, as now conducted in the best
Schools, is no longer simply drawing. All the
various courses are based on the study of models
and objects, and include not only form study and
drawing, but clay modelling, paper-folding and
cutting, and the making of models and objects in
various materials. The instruction given has a
direct bearing on manual training, and much attention is paid to the connection of drawing with other
studies, and its helpfulness in all lines of school
work.

" All thorough work in drawing being based upon
the study of form in objects, the Prang courses pro-

vide first of all for the placing of well-chosen models
in the hands of school-children, from the lowest
primary grade upward. This is done in order that
pupils may become clearly and accurately acquainted
with—

" (*a*) The facts of form,

" (*b*) The appearance of form,

and be prepared to reproduce their knowledge by
the two methods of—

" (*a*) Constructive drawing and—

" (*b*) Representative drawing.

" The courses provide also for thorough instruction in the principles of decoration, and expression
of the knowledge obtained by decorative drawing."

Side by side with this comes the effort to develop
colour, and I again quote from their pamphlets :—

" Extended and careful observations of young
children, made by competent persons under the
most varied conditions, show it to be a fact that
children do not see colour as adults see colour. The
colour sense in most young children is imperfect in
action and limited in range. The Prang course of
instruction in colour begins by recognising this fact,
and appeals, in the first place, to the child's rudi-
mentary colour sense. From this beginning it

unfolds through graded exercises, involving at every step the activity of the pupil's individual powers of colour observation and colour expression. The object of these exercises is—

"To develop in the pupil, through direct and repeated observation of colour, the power to recognise beauty and harmony in colour effects.

"To train the pupil, through the wisely guided personal use of colour material, to skill in expressing thought and feeling by the use of such material.

"To so connect the pupil's study of colour with that of form, drawing, and other branches of school instruction that his developing powers of colour observation and colour expression may be of value in his study of nature and of art."

In some schools the Prang system of teaching drawing is followed closely; in others a system based upon the Prang system is used; but in most of the Schools which I saw the influence of the system seemed to me apparent, even where the system itself had been discarded.

In one school I visited, the teacher of drawing had taught on the Prang system; but this year had been allowed liberty, and had tried various experiments with success, amongst others illustrating poems such as Wordsworth's " Poor Susan."

Drawing is frequently begun from the first year of the school life. The children are early trained to draw from nature : grass, radishes, and leaves and flowers picked from the woods were being drawn in various classes ; the grass, with its root, being drawn by children of eight, the radish by children of about ten.

In Washington girls of thirteen or fourteen were drawing a plant very creditably, yet were receiving no particular directions.

Drawing at the Pratt Institute, Brooklyn, is based on the Prang system of drawing, and graduates of Class B in the Prang system may take the full course at the Pratt Institute.

In one school—Lincoln School, Philadelphia—the first primary grade children were sent to the board in groups of fifteen to twenty to draw large circles in chalk, first with right hand, then with left, and finally with both hands at the same time, the object being to give freedom of movement while the child is young.

The instruction in drawing is so arranged as to carry on simultaneously three lines of development :

**F**

(*a*) The study of form, by handling the objects and then representing them on paper. This is done largely by the handling of small models and by clay modelling, and is continued till the children are twelve or thirteen years of age.

(*b*) Construction, *i.e.*, the representation in drawing of the various surfaces of an object—say a cube, a plinth, etc.—with measurements which would be required by a mechanic.

(*c*) Designing, when the forms studied are multi-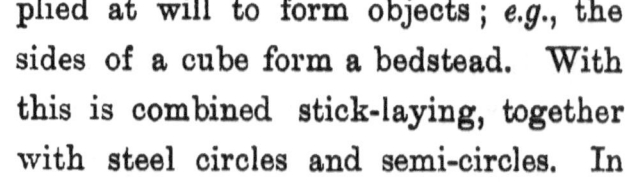plied at will to form objects ; *e.g.*, the sides of a cube form a bedstead. With this is combined stick-laying, together with steel circles and semi-circles. In one class where this was being done the children 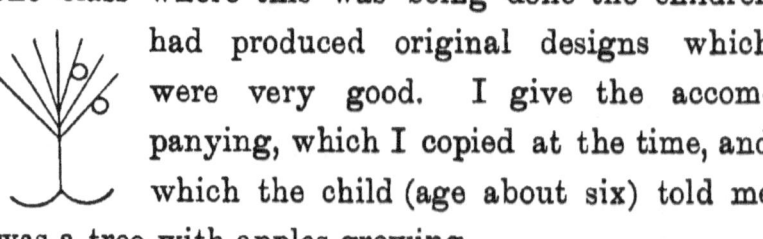had produced original designs which were very good. I give the accompanying, which I copied at the time, and which the child (age about six) told me was a tree with apples growing.

In the same School drawing is made to enter into almost every department of school teaching. No history lesson is given without a sketch of the district concerned being drawn, while in geography clay models are made to illustrate geographical terms, and maps are made with sand.

In conclusion, I may say that I should judge the time allotted to drawing, particularly in the younger grades, is wise, and the plans for teaching drawing carefully thought out; but one point struck me as being weak—namely, that all grade teachers, irrespective of previous training and apart from talent, or even capacity for drawing, or appreciation of colour, have to teach drawing; for instance, in one school I specially noticed how the class reflected the lack of training in the teacher. No trained teacher of drawing would have failed to call attention to the way in which leaves grow out of a stalk; but in this school most curious representations of such growth were allowed to pass uncorrected. I must, however, in justice say that in several cities the plan of appointing supervisors of drawing is being adopted, and this will no doubt in some measure remedy this weakness.

# LIST OF INTERVIEWS,

## ALSO OF

## INSTITUTIONS VISITED.

| Place. | Institutions. | Interviews. |
|---|---|---|
| * Brooklyn. | | Dr. Maxwell (School Superintendent). |
| | Girls' High School. | Mr. Patterson (Principal). |
| | | Prof. Spice (Professor of Science in Girls' High School, also member of Faculty of Coopers' Union). |
| | | Miss Blanding (Vice-Principal of High School). |
| | No. 52, Ellery Street. | Miss Emily Black (Principal). |
| | No. 74, Kosciusko Street. | Misses Franklin and Irvine. |
| | Packer Institution. | Dr. Backus (Principal). |
| | Pratt Institute. | Miss Bird (Registrar). |
| | Pratt High School. | |
| Vassar. | The College. | President Taylor. |
| | | Mrs. Kendal (Lady Superintendent and teachers on the staff). |
| Springfield. | Schools closed for spring vacation. | Mr. Wood (Clerk to Superintendent). |
| Northampton. | Smith College. | L. Clark Seelye, Esq. (President), also the Secretary. |
| | Centre Primary School (Training School). | Miss Kingsley and teachers in charge. |
| Boston. | | Mr. Seaver (School Superintendent). |
| | Girls' High School. | Mr. Tetlow (Principal). |

| Place. | Institutions. | Interviews. |
|---|---|---|
| Boston (continued). | Girls' Latin School. | |
| | Prince School. | Dr. Young (Principal). |
| | Normal School building. | A teacher. |
| | Students out visiting schools. | |
| | Rice Schools. | |
| | Slöjd School. | Mr. Gustav Larsson (teacher of Normal School Slöjd). |
| | Mrs. Hemenway's Gymnasium. | Dr. Enebuske (Director of Gymnasium). Miss Homans (representative of Mrs. Hemenway). |
| | Technological Institute. | General Walker (Principal). |
| | Headquarters of Prang Drawing Company. | Lady in charge (name not caught). |
| | Wellesley College. | Miss Whiting (head of Science Department). Miss Tuttle and Miss Pendreton (the latter of Newnham). |
| | Mrs. Quincey Shaw's Kindergarten. | Various teachers. |
| Philadelphia. | Board of Education meeting. | Dr. Brooks (School Superintendent). Miss Wright (Assistant Superintendent). |
| | Private Training College for teachers in Kindergarten and Schools. | Miss Stewart (friend of Miss Graeff and head of private college, also appointed by State of Pennsylvania to represent State in Educational Department at Chicago Exhibition). |
| | Landreth School. | Miss Wallis (Principal). |
| | Lincoln School. | Miss Cross (Principal). |
| Washington. | Bureau of Education. | Dr. Harris (Commissioner of Education). |

| Place. | Institutions. | Interviews. |
|---|---|---|
| Washington (continued). | | Miss Smith(assistant in charge of English and French departments). General Eaton (ex-Commissioner). |
| | Franklin School. | Mr. Powell (School Superintendent). |
| | Normal Training School. | The Clerk of Superintendent and a teacher of the Normal School. |
| | Manual Training School. (*a*) Cookery School. (*b*)Carpentry School. (*c*) Turning lathes and machinery. | |
| | High School. Polk School. Henry Grammar School. | Dr. Lane (Principal). |
| | Wayland Seminary (coloured students). | Miss Jewett (assistant teacher). |
| * Indianapolis. | | Mr. Jones (School Superintendent). Miss Cropsey (Assistant Superintendent). |
| | School No. 2. | Miss Hamilton (Principal of School). |
| | School No. 11. School No. 32. School No. 10. High School. Normal School. | Miss Kirlin (Principal). |
| St. Louis. | | Miss Nicholson (Principal of Training Department). Dr. Long (School Superintendent). Miss McClure. |
| | Franklin School. | |

| Place. | Institutions. | Interviews. |
|---|---|---|
| St. Louis (continued). | Jefferson School. | |
| Leavenworth, Kansas. | | Mr. Klock (School Superintendent). |
| | High School. | Mr. Evans (Principal). Miss Scott (a teacher). |
| | Morris School. Oak Street School. Coloured School. | |
| Omaha, Nebraska. | | Mr. Fitzpatrick (School Superintendent). |
| | Kellom School. | Miss Foos (Principal). |
| | Farnam School. | Miss Truland (Principal). |
| Denver. | | Mr. Beggs (School Superintendent *pro tem.*). |
| | Wyman School. | Mr. Long (Principal). Miss Alderman and other teachers. |
| | High School. | Teachers on the staff. |
| | Longfellow School. | Mr. Elder (Principal). |
| | Emerson School Corona      „ Whittier    „ Hyde Park „ Gilpin       „ | Brief interviews with the Principal of each building. |
| Manitou. | School building. | Mr. Barker (Secretary of Board of Education). |
| Chicago. | | Mr. Sabin (Assistant School Superintendent). |
| | Schools closed for vacation. | |
| | Attended Chicago University Convocation meetings. | J. Shortall, Esq. |
| | Studied American educational exhibits at World's Fair. | |

* Schools in Brooklyn City and in Indianapolis are known by their numbers which were given them in the order in which they were built.

www.ingramcontent.com/pod-product-compliance
Lightning Source LLC
Chambersburg PA
CBHW032356020726
47499CB00008B/2768